2.95
#18

11/30/2019

Wishing You a
Happy, Successful, Incredible Life!

Christian

This book says it all. It's a true map and helpful guide through your entire life. Every page is filled with Hope, Truth and words of Wisdom.
God Blessed me with the most fabulous and handsome Grandson in this entire world, and for this, I give thanks to God every day. Happy 16th Birthday dear.
My Love for ever,
from, Grandma Suzanne

Wishing You a
Happy, Successful,
Incredible Life!

Positive words about
all the things that matter most

Douglas Pagels

Blue Mountain Press™
Boulder, Colorado

Library of Congress Control Number: 2013941832
ISBN: 978-1-59842-759-2

▌and Blue Mountain Press are registered in U.S. Patent and Trademark Office.
Certain trademarks are used under license.

Printed in China.
First Printing: 2013

✪ This book is printed on recycled paper.

This book is printed on paper that has been specially produced to be acid free (neutral pH) and contains no groundwood or unbleached pulp. It conforms with the requirements of the American National Standards Institute, Inc., so as to ensure that this book will last and be enjoyed by future generations.

Blue Mountain Arts, Inc.

P.O. Box 4549, Boulder, Colorado 80306

Contents

You Have So Much to Look Forward To

You have so many wonderful days ahead of you! Each morning of your life is part of your journey, and the path you are on is one that will help you become all that you were meant to be.

Each moment brings you a little closer... to reaching your potential, realizing your dreams, and discovering all those things that make you smile inside.

Welcome to the happy, successful, incredible life...

   that is waiting just for you.

I may be uncertain about exactly where I'm headed, but I am very clear regarding this:

I'm glad I've got a ticket to go on this magnificent journey.

I hope your dreams take you...
to the corners of your smiles,
to the highest of your hopes,
to the windows of your opportunities,
and to the most special places
your heart has ever known.

It All
Circles Around

*S*uccess is so much more than most people imagine it to be. Success is looking forward to the day. It's having plans and wishes and goals to go after. It's letting your heart say yes.

Success is a reflection of happiness.

Happiness is the reward you receive for living well.

Living well comes from doing all you possibly can to have days that are rich and full... and a journey that is blessed.

And being blessed?

Now that's the sweetest success.

*W*ant to know the real secret of getting rich? It's easy... you just need to remember this:

Friendships are priceless, time is invaluable, health is wealth, and love is a treasure.

Count your blessings. Invest in your dreams. Profit from experience. Share your good fortune.

And spend your hours wisely each day.

Someday we'll all look back at our lives
and realize that it's actually kind of funny...
discovering that the things we valued most
had absolutely nothing to do
    ...with money.

Good News About Your Future

Don't spend too much time looking in the rearview mirror. Yesterday is behind you. What's done is done, and it's important to take what you've learned from the experience and just move on...

Today is a brand-new opportunity,
a blank canvas, an unwritten page...
just waiting to see. All that needs
to happen right now is for you...
to do the amazing things you're
capable of.

And tomorrow? That's the place
where promises come true. You'll
need to be smart and stay strong to
live the life you want to have.

But don't ever forget: you are
creative and capable and wise,
and I know you have what
it takes to make your days
everything you want them to be.
And remember this for sure:

You can't change a single thing
about the past, but you can
change absolutely everything
about the future.

Success Is Found in the Little Things You Do Every Day

I want you to learn, laugh, grow, dream, discover, and reach. I want you to choose wisely, be strong, and keep on being the remarkable person you are.

Be someone who doesn't make your guardian angel work too hard or worry too much.

*Have connections with others
that are natural and easy
and comfortable and kind...*

Remember that the more you use the Golden Rule (you know... do unto others as though you were the others), the brighter your days will shine.

Always keep the lines of communication open. People may need only a little, but they need that little a lot.

And never forget: each new day is a blank page in the diary of your life. Every day, you're given a chance to determine what the words will say and how the story will unfold. The more rewarding you can make each page, the more amazing the entire book will be.

And I would love for you to write
 a masterpiece.

Always Be
Be Hope-Full

To have hope in your life is exactly what it's like for the night to have stars in the sky.

It's a brilliant way to be.

And among all those stars and all those wishes waiting to come true, I have so many wishes for you. I want you to have the strength and courage to see your way through anything. I want life to bring you all the good things and special days you deserve.

*D*ecisions are incredibly important things!
Good decisions will come back to bless you.
Bad decisions can come back to haunt you.

That's why it's so important that you take the
time to choose wisely.

Choose to do the things that will reflect well...
on your ability, your integrity, your spirit, your
health, your tomorrows, your smiles, your dreams,
and yourself.

There is someone who will thank you for doing the things you do now with foresight and wisdom and respect.

It's the person you will someday be.

You have a chance to make that person so thankful and so proud. All you have to do is remember these nine little words:

> Each time you come to a crossroads
> ...choose wisely.

Daily Readings to Make Your Life the Best It Can Be

Monday: Shine bright enough to light your way and sparkle whenever you can.

Tuesday: Remember what they say, "Each day is a gift. That's why we call it the present."

Wednesday: Let joy, excitement, reverence,
and grace all have a place in your life...

Thursday: Don't just have minutes in the day. Have moments in time.

Friday: Be well dressed. Laugh your socks off and wear a smile wherever you go.

Saturday: *Realize that you can always find a way to see things through.*

Someday: *And always remember: the very best dreams... are the ones you make come true.*

What Do You Want to Be When You Grow Up?

When we're young, people ask us that question a lot. When we're older... not so much.

But even though we may be a few – or quite a few – years away from childhood, it doesn't mean we're all grown up.

Even for those of us who have been around awhile, the "what do you want to be?" question is still valid – and today's answers are much more insightful than they were when we were kids...

Our answers now have less to do with owning a unicorn, shooting through space, or being a rock star... and more to do with attainable dreams, day-to-day things, and serenity and happiness.

What do I want to be when I grow up?

Here are a few of my goals... and if you want to incorporate any of them into yours, you're more than welcome to.

When I grow up, I want to make sure that my future self (the 2.0 version of me) is a reflection of the person I truly want to be...

I want to take every necessary step and do every positive thing in my power to make that happen. And I know that it may take some time, but I'll get there.

I am not going to settle for less and let life just pass me by. I am going to share those smiles and make those memories and do those things I want to do.

When I grow up, I'm going to be the best "me" that I can possibly be.

If You Do
These Ten Things...

You Will Be Able to See Your Way
Through Just About Anything

*S*tay positive! (Hopeful people are happier
people.) ⇐ Choose wisely. (Good choices
will come back to bless you.) ⇐ Remember
what matters. (The present moment. The good
people in it. Hopes and dreams and feelings.)

≪ Don't stress out over things you can't control. (Just don't.) ≪ Count every blessing. (Even the little ones add up to a lot.) ≪ Be good to your body. (It's the only one you get.) ≪ Listen to the wishes of your heart. (It always seems to know what's true, what's right, what to do, and where to go with your life.)...

⤟ Understand how special you are.
⤟ Realize how strong you can be.

⤝ And know that, YES, you're going to make it through, no matter what.

Maybe you won't be dancing in the streets or jumping on the bed... but you are going to get through the day, the night, and each and every moment that lies ahead. (I promise.)

Everyone Is Entitled to a Do-Over

*I*f – for any reason – "last year's you" wasn't the person you aspired to be... or if you didn't get far enough along on the list of hopes and goals you wanted to achieve...

Lucky you. You get a second chance!

All you have to do is resolve to take "this year's you" and turn that person into more of who you want to be.

So much of life is just a matter of setting priorities, staying the course, and reaching the desired outcome.

Good to Know

Having a wish list is good.

Having a checklist... is great.

(Note to self: It's always best to get motivated and take action. Just being able to check items off the list gives you a real sense of accomplishment.)

If each day is too short for all the wonderful things you want to do, don't be frustrated.

Be thankful... that your wish list is so full.

You Get to Choose...
(but only one choice has less stress)

Living in the "here and now" is always the best option for how to live your life.

But if you'd rather try living in the "there and then," you don't need an appointment. Your regrets over the past and your worries over the future will be happy to squeeze you in.

There are times in life when just being brave is all you need to be.

You may not always know what to do next... or how to get where you're going in life, but if you just stay strong, trust in your faith, and make the very best choices you possibly can, a few things may not go as planned... but almost everything else will work out right.

I Wish Every Success... for You!

Success doesn't have an agenda to follow.

There are no milestones you have to reach. There's no expiration date you have to worry about... or any deadline that dictates whether you've "made it" or not...

Success isn't an exclusive club that only a privileged few are invited to join. It isn't found in a big house, a fancy car, or a lavish lifestyle. It has nothing to do with where you went to school, whether you have the latest version of this and the greatest model of that, or how much you accumulate in your lifetime.

*There are a hundred things that success
is not, but only a few precious things
that it actually is.*

*To me, success has implications that
reach from deep in the heart to very
high up in the sky, and it involves hopes
and prayers that wish you blessings too
wonderful for words...*

Your well-being is the foundation that everything rests upon.

If you have a strong foundation of family and friends, a level of health (physically and emotionally) that is the very best you can achieve, treasured memories to look back upon, beautiful hopes to look forward to, and if you're able to provide your heart and soul with the kinds of things that bring them joy and serenity, then you will have achieved a measure of success that is enviable and admirable.

My heartfelt wish for you is...
may you be so blessed.

Happiness isn't having the ideal everything. Perfection is unattainable.

If you want to be truly joyful and grateful and fulfilled on a daily basis, simply gravitate toward those special things and precious memories... that make your heart smile.

That kind of happiness is wonderful and rewarding and sustainable.

You ou are personally responsible for so much of the sunshine that brightens up your life. Optimists and gentle souls continually benefit from their very own versions of daylight saving time. They get extra hours of happiness and sunshine every day.

Celebrate Your Uniqueness

You are something – and someone – very special.

You really are. No one else in this entire world is exactly like you, and there are so many beautiful things about you. You're a one-of-a-kind treasure, uniquely here in this space and time. You are here to shine in your own wonderful way, sharing your smile in the best way you can, and remembering all the while that a little light somewhere makes a brighter light everywhere. You can — and you do — make a wonderful contribution to this world.

These Are the Gifts
I Wish for You

The gift of knowing that it's
people like you who make life
so much better.

All your friends and loved ones,
from close by and miles away,
finding a moment in the day to
be thankful for you.

Happiness that simply overflows...
from memories made, peacefulness
within, and the anticipation of so
many good things to come.

Days that shine so bright and wishing
stars that come out at night and listen
to everything your heart is hoping for...

I wish you paths ahead that take you all the places you want to be and that bring you closer to all the great things you deserve.

The kind of joy that you always give to others... coming back to bless you all through the year.

And reminders that in so many ways, you are such a wonderful gift, and...

...one of the nicest things in this entire world
is your presence in it.

Some Assembly Is Required

*M*ost of us have a put-together life, rather than one that has effortlessly blossomed into what it is today.

Every new day brings us changes and gives us chances... to revise and rebuild, take away from, add to, and make our life take the kind of shape we want it to.

When we're putting our lives together, let's have them – please – consist of these things...

A sense of ourselves. An appreciation for how completely unique we are. The absolute best kind of connections. The luxury of true friendship and reciprocal love. Caring. Understanding and grace. And the wisdom to always listen to what our hearts are trying to say.

Practice Your Tree Pose

I want you to have a wonderful understanding of who you are... and a strong sense of your place in the world.

I want you to be nourished in body and
soul, and I want you to go through the
days ahead with greater self-acceptance
and a goal of finding a way to bring
everything in your life into balance.

Let the roots of all your dreams go deep.
Let the hopes of all your tomorrows
    grow high.
Bend, but don't break.
Take the seasons as they come.
Stick up for yourself.

And reach for the sky.

Be Open to the Possibilities

I want you to refrain from putting any limits on yourself. I want you to be amazed at what you discover you can do.

Limitations are less than desirable things. You can't go through life with restrictions on how much you can accomplish.

There shouldn't be any boundaries on how unique and remarkable you can be. And if you want to welcome in those sudden, wonderful insights and exclamation-point moments, you can't close yourself off to all that creativity inside you.

In order to have a truly rewarding life, you've got to be open to the possibilities!

This is a totally uneducated guess, but I'm just going to have to bet that people with willing hearts have many more great days, more fun encounters, and much more meaningful connections with other people...

And I can easily imagine that those who have open minds get more of the good stuff... opportunities that come knocking, sweet people who come calling, and nice surprises that stop by to say hello.

When a new morning begins your day and you're mentally projecting into the hours ahead, don't ever think in terms of "this is exactly how it's going to be."

Always think in terms of "even ordinary days can have extraordinary touches to them... and anything can happen... so let's just wait and see"...

Things that happen serendipitously are those that seem – at first glance – to occur for no apparent reason. But then – after further reflection – it's as if they were meant to be. The little miracles and magic moments in our lives need willing hearts, open minds, and a little serendipity to help them appear.

So, yes. Invite those moments in by being someone who believes in possibilities and who never closes off to what might be just around the bend. Be open to those magical, unexpected things.

They can make your life incredible and exceptional and a lot more interesting.

Keep Chasing Your Dreams and Don't Stop Until You Catch Them

There are things you would like to do in your life. There are dreams you wish would come true in your life. There are goals you want to reach, places you want to go, and things you hope to accomplish.

There are people to meet, friends to make, and feelings of love you want to have in your heart...

There are so many wishes and desires
that are a wonderful part of who you are.

Those things... are your dreams.

They're the things that fill your life with
hope and happiness and that make your
days rewarding and simply amazing.

Never let go of your dreams. Keep
wanting them, working for them, and
believing in them. Be strong and steady
and devoted.

And never forget... on your journey
through life, you will one day see...
your accomplishments will far surpass
any disappointments, your successes
will triumph over any failures, and
your dreams will bring you smiles and
blessings and beautiful things... that
you haven't even dreamed of yet.

Just Tune In

If we take the time to listen, sometimes we hear little whispers and wondrous insights that give us clues on what it's going to take to make our days happier and our lives richer.

Don't ever ignore those little insights you hear. They're filled with hope and love and care... and they're usually quite important and wonderfully true.

The big question is... what is your heart telling you?...

Sometimes your head and your heart get together and they come up with something they just have to pass along to you... right this minute... about a special feeling, a particular person, or a certain situation.

Sometimes it seems like the answers we need just come from out of the blue. But... that's not really how it is. It's more like a process where you put the question out there in the universe... and the universe gets back to you with an answer.

Regardless of how it happens, it's a remarkable thing. It's a bit of intuition and a little magic combined, and it provides you with a really remarkable kind of insider information.

Wise people pay attention to those types of things. So don't ever be too busy to tune in when your heart has something it needs to share with you. Who knows? That one thing might be the thing that makes all the difference.

Some "Life Advice" to Always Remember

*N*othing ever has and no one ever will compare with you. You deserve to be happy, to love yourself, and to be able to live your very best life... every day.

Don't ever believe anyone who tells you otherwise. You matter immensely. Your wishes are so important. Your hopes and dreams are valid and valuable. And your inner strength is more powerful than you can imagine...

Never give up on the things you want to come true. Take what you want to do and need to do... and reach for it.

Life has so much to give when you hope and love and live each day in the very best way you can. There are no limits to the good you can do and the smiles you can bring to your heart.

You're entitled to all the great things that come your way. You are amazing and capable and just so exquisite.

And when it comes to a wonderful life, one that brings all the best things to you, I want you to know how much you deserve it.

How to Earn Extra Credit in the School of Life

By virtue of being a living, breathing, thinking human being on this planet, you are automatically enrolled in a never-ending learning process. Classes start again each day, and a little homework, although it is sometimes optional, is expected of everyone.

The assignments in the school of life always focus on what to do, how to do it, and what it takes to get it right. Here are a few things you can do to earn extra credit...

Do what you love.
Live with a little bravado.
Think of what inspires you most.

Spend less time in the whirlwind
of life... and more time in the calm.

Have days that make your spirit soar
and your heart sing.

Have at least a dozen things you're
passionate about.

Remember that every time you give someone
    a lasting smile, you get one back.

Be generous.

Dress for success – do things that suit your needs.
Be wealthy – have a rich imagination.

Whenever things are tough, make the vow,
    "I'll get through this."
And then... don't let <u>anything</u> get in the
    way of following up on that promise...

Keep your balance.
Drink your water.
Listen to what your fortune cookies
   are telling you.

Remember that a new morning is
good medicine... and one of the
blessings of life is having a daily dose
of all the amazing things this world
has to give.

Give thanks. Endlessly.

Always have good intentions.
Find comfort in knowing that "rising above"
    is something you can find a way to do.

Be tremendously less concerned
    about what others think of you...

Look up "onward" in the thesaurus
and utilize every one of those synonyms
whenever you're wondering which
direction to go in.

Think less and imagine more.
See less and envision more.
Be curious and learn more.

Be bighearted and open-minded.

Don't judge yourself – love yourself.
Savor the little gifts of grace.

Always have something to look forward to.

If you have the choice between a
la-di-da life and an ooh-la-la one,
well... you know what to do.

Choose the one that requires you
    to dust off your dancing shoes...

And for the most extra credit of all,
    be sure to do this:

Start by finding a nice sheet of paper
    and your very best pen.
Then... get lost in your thoughts and
    write out <u>your</u> definition of success.

Fill it with a mix of stardust and wishes
and down-to-earth things, and provide
all the insight you can give it.

Imagine what it takes to have a happy life.

And then go out... and live it.

About the Author

Best-selling author and editor Douglas Pagels has inspired millions of readers with his insights and his anthologies. His books have sold over 3 million copies, and he is one of the most quoted contemporary writers on the Internet today. Reflecting  a philosophy that is perfect for our times, Doug has a wonderful knack for sharing his thoughts and sentiments in a voice that is so positive and understanding we can't help but take the message to heart.

His writings have been translated into over a dozen languages due to their global appeal and inspiring outlook on life, and his work has been quoted by many worthy causes and charitable organizations.

He and his wife live in Colorado, and they are the parents of children in college and beyond. Over the years, Doug has spent much of his time as a classroom volunteer, a youth basketball coach, an advocate for local environmental issues, a frequent traveler, and a craftsman, building a cabin in the Rocky Mountains.